$34.00

CUTTING EDGE MEDICINE

In Vitro Fertilization

Steve Parker

WORLD ALMANAC® LIBRARY

Please visit our Web site at: **www.garethstevens.com**
For a free color catalog describing World Almanac® Library's list of high-quality books
and multimedia programs, call 1-800-848-2928 (USA) or 1-800-387-3178 (Canada).
World Almanac® Library's fax: (414) 332-3567.

Library of Congress Cataloging-in-Publication Data available upon request from publisher.
Fax (414) 336-0157 for the attention of the Publishing Records Department.

ISBN 978-0-8368-7866-0 (lib. bdg.)

This North American edition first published in 2007 by
World Almanac® Library
A Member of the WRC Media Family of Companies
330 West Olive Street, Suite 100
Milwaukee, WI 53212 USA

This U.S. edition copyright © 2007 by World Almanac® Library.
Original edition copyright © 2007 by Arcturus Publishing Limited.

Produced by Arcturus Publishing Limited.
Editor: Alex Woolf
Designer: Nick Phipps
Consultant: Dr. Eleanor Clarke

World Almanac® Library editor: Carol Ryback
World Almanac® Library designer: Kami M. Strunsee
World Almanac® Library art direction: Tammy West
World Almanac® Library production: Jessica Yanke and Robert Kraus

The right of Andrew Solway to be identified as the author of this work has been
asserted by him in accordance with the Copyright, Designs and Patents Act, 1988.

Photo credits: CORBIS: / Tomas Van Houtryve 35; / Shawn Thew/epa 53. Getty Images: / Time Life Pictures 16; /
18. Michael Courtney: / 6, 9. Rex Features: / Action Press 36; / Mark St. George 51; / Jon Freeman 59. Science
Photo Library: / D. Phillips cover, 11; / Hank Morgan 5, 31, 38; / Steve Allen 12; / AJ Photo 15, 21; / SCIMAT 23,
25; / BSIP 26; / Pascal Goetgheluck 28, 57; / Zephyr 33; / BSIP / Laurent 41; / John Howard 43; / Adam Gault 45;
/ Andrew Syred 46; / Mauro Fermariello 48; / James King-Holmes 55.

Printed in China

1 2 3 4 5 6 7 8 9 10 10 09 08 07 06

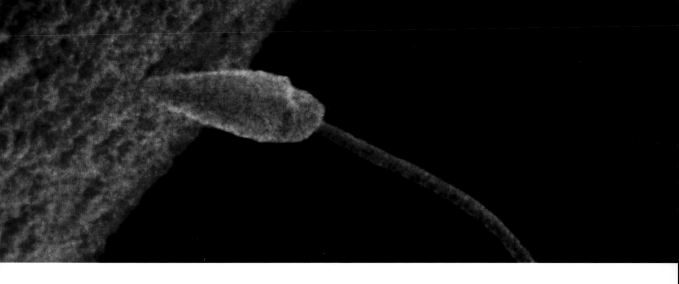

Contents

CHAPTER 1

What Is In Vitro Fertilization?

In vitro fertilization, or IVF, is a process in which a woman's egg is joined with a man's sperm outside the body in order to create a baby. *In vitro* is Latin for "in glass." Fertilization is a stage in breeding or reproduction—the process of making babies. IVF, or "fertilization in glass," refers to medical and laboratory containers such as flasks or test tubes. In fact, the container is more likely to be a flat, circular dish called a petri dish, and may well be made out of plastic rather than glass. Even so, the process is still called IVF.

Basics of IVF

IVF is an artificial way to start, or conceive, a baby. The natural way to start a baby is for a man's sperm to enter a woman's body during sexual intercourse and for the sperm to then fertilize one of the

CUTTING EDGE MOMENTS

The discovery of human sperm

Until the seventeenth century, people had no idea that eggs and sperm existed. There were no microscopes to make them visible. Anton van Leeuwenhoek (1632–1723) was a Dutch textile merchant and amateur scientist. In the early 1670s, he began developing magnifying lenses. He drew pictures and wrote descriptions of the tiny life forms he discovered in this previously unseen world. In 1677, he described sperm cells from a dog. Later, he observed human sperm: "A large number of small animalcules, I think it must be more than a thousand, on an area no larger than a grain of sand." Van Leeuwenhoek's discoveries opened the way to a new area of human biology and medicine, including a greater understanding of reproduction.

woman's eggs. In other words, a sperm cell unites with an egg cell to enable the development of a baby. The fertilized egg then develops inside the woman's uterus into a baby, which is born nine months later. For a more detailed description of human reproduction, see pages 6 to 13.

In IVF, eggs are removed from the woman, and sperm is removed from the man. The eggs and sperm are then combined in a container so that fertilization can occur. A fertilized egg that results is put back into the woman's uterus so that it can grow and develop into a baby. With IVF, fertilization happens in artificial surroundings, rather than in a woman's body. For a more detailed description of the process of IVF, see Chapter 3 (*pages 20–33*).

Droplets of sperm are added to a petri dish containing ripe eggs in order to fertilize them—part of the process of in vitro fertilization.

IVF and ART

IVF is one of several methods known as assisted reproductive technologies, or ARTs. These are scientific methods of helping people have children. The process of reproduction can be aided or assisted at various stages, depending on the problems of those wanting a baby. In some cases, IVF alone is advised. In other cases, IVF may be combined with other methods (*see pages 32–33*).

Human reproduction

To understand how IVF works requires some knowledge of the reproductive process—how humans make babies. This, in turn, cannot be understood without some information about basic human biology.

This diagram shows the organs of the female reproductive system.

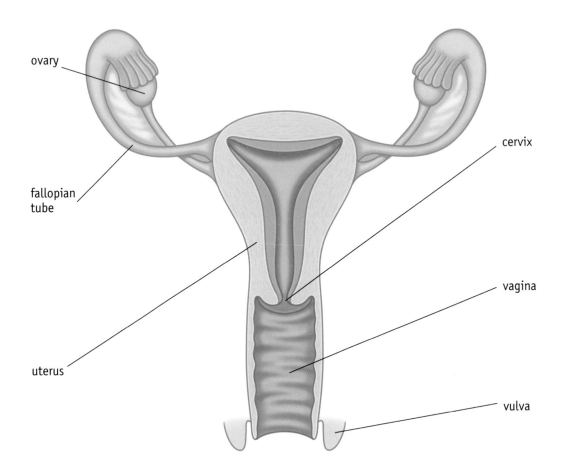

ovary

cervix

fallopian tube

vagina

uterus

vulva

The human body is made of billions of tiny "building blocks" called cells. There are many different kinds of cells, including nerve cells, blood cells, bone cells, and brain cells. Most are so small that countless numbers of them would fit on a pinhead. Two special types of cell are needed to start a baby. These are an egg cell from a woman and a sperm cell from a man. They are made by the reproductive organs.

Eggs and ovaries

A woman's body contains more than a quarter of a million egg cells. They are located in two organs, called ovaries, in her lower abdomen, one on each side of the uterus. Every month or so, one egg follicle in one of the ovaries becomes ripe and ready for fertilization. The bodily changes that make the egg follicle ripen are called the menstrual cycle. The changes are controlled by hormones, natural chemical substances that travel around in the blood and affect how the body functions.

At the follicle's ripest time, the ends of the fallopian tube fold around the ovary to catch the egg, which bursts from the follicle— a process called ovulation. The egg, which is about one-tenth of a millimeter in diameter, begins its journey toward the uterus. Once ovulation occurs, the woman's internal body conditions will only allow fertilization for two or three days. Fertilization usually occurs in the fallopian tubes. Whether or not fertilization occurs, the egg continues to move through the fallopian tube toward the uterus.

CUTTING EDGE MOMENTS

Fertility drugs

Fertility means being capable of reproducing. Women can take fertility drugs so that their ovaries are more likely to release ripe eggs. The first fertility drug was produced in 1949 at the Istituto Farmacologico Serono (IFS) in Rome, Italy, by Piero Donini. It contained substances called gonadotropins, produced by a tiny gland under the brain called the pituitary gland. The gonadotropins travel around the body in the blood and affect the ovaries, which encourage an egg to ripen. Modern laboratory-made versions of these drugs are now common in all kinds of IVF and fertility work.

Each ripe egg is released from a small fluid-filled container in the ovary, called a follicle. Before the egg is released, the follicle produces the female hormones estrogen and progesterone. These hormones cause the lining of the uterus, known as the endometrium, to become soft, thickened, and rich in blood. This readies the uterus so it can nourish the fetus as it develops from the fertilized egg.

After the egg leaves the follicle, the empty follicle changes into a small yellowish lump, the corpus luteum. This continues to produce estrogen and progesterone, causing the endometrium to become still thicker, as the egg drifts along the fallopian tube.

If the egg is not fertilized, the corpus luteum gradually breaks down. Without the corpus luteum's hormones, the blood-rich uterus lining breaks down, too. This occurs around twelve to fourteen days after release of the egg. The pieces of uterus lining pass through the opening or neck of the uterus, called the cervix. They then leave the body through a tube called the vagina, or birth canal. This loss of blood-rich uterus lining from the vagina is known as menstruation, or having a period.

A few days later, still under the control of the female hormones, a new egg starts to ripen. Then, the whole series of changes that make up the menstrual cycle begins again.

CUTTING EDGE   SCIENTISTS

Gabriele Fallopius

Gabriele Fallopius (Gabriello Falloppio, 1523–1562) was an early scientific anatomist—an expert in the body's structure. By careful dissection (cutting open) of dead bodies, Fallopius discovered detailed structures in the skull, ear, and in the female reproductive organs. In 1561, he described the tubes from the ovaries to the uterus, now called the fallopian tubes.

Sperm and testicles

The male reproductive organs are in the lower abdomen and below the abdomen. Two of these organs, the testicles (or testes), produce sperm cells. The testicles hang outside a man's body, below the abdomen, in a skin bag called the scrotum. Sperm cells are tadpole-shaped, with a rounded head and a long, whippy tail. Each day, hundreds of millions of new sperm cells are produced. They are stored in the epididymides, two tightly coiled, 20-foot (6-meter) -long tubes next to each testicle.

Sperm leave the man's body through a series of tubes. Muscle spasms push the sperm from each testicle and epididymis into a tube called the vas deferens, or sperm duct. In the man's lower abdomen, the two sperm ducts join another tube, the urethra, that runs through the penis. The sperm travel through the urethra (inside the penis) and out of the end of the penis.

This diagram shows the organs of the male reproductive system.

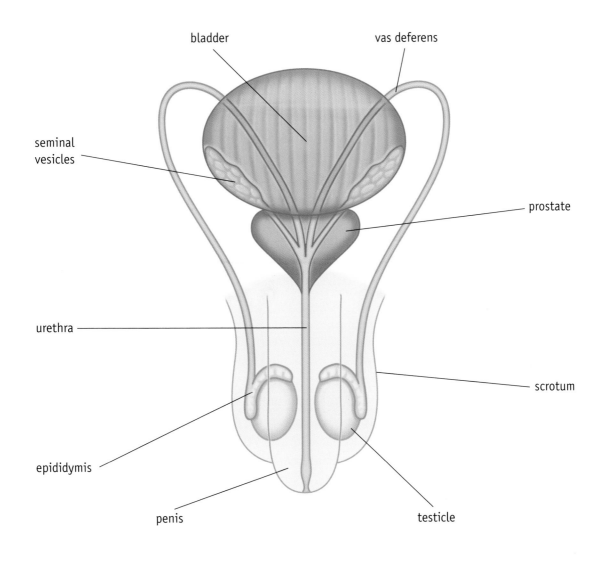

The sperm leave the body in a milky liquid, called seminal fluid, produced by the prostate gland and the seminal vesicles. Sperm in seminal fluid are known as semen. Any sperm that are not expelled from the body die and break apart harmlessly within the testicles and epididymides, and the man's body reabsorbs them.

CUTTING EDGE   FACTS

Sperm and egg cells

Sperm cells are much smaller than egg cells. Each sperm is about one-twentieth of 1 mm long. It consists basically of a "head" and a "tail." A round egg cell, meanwhile, is about one-tenth of 1 mm in diameter. The volume of each egg cell is hundreds of times larger than that of a sperm cell.

More than two hundred years ago, people thought that the head of a sperm contained a curled up human body. They believed the woman's role was simply to provide a place for this tiny body to grow. We now know that egg and sperm each contribute the same amount of genetic material, or DNA, to the baby.

Sperm movement in the seminal fluid

Seminal fluid that leaves the man's body and enters the woman's body contains more that two hundred million sperm in one teaspoonful (5 milliliters) of fluid. The tails of the sperm propel them up into the woman's uterus. Then, they continue swimming into either of the two fallopian tubes, to the left or right.

Fertilization

If a ripe egg is waiting in one of the fallopian tubes, many sperm surround it. Hundreds of sperm bombard the egg until one finally penetrates the egg's membrane, or outer covering. As the membrane opens, the DNA in the sperm's head unites with the DNA of the egg cell. At this instant, the egg is fertilized.

It only takes one sperm to fertilize an egg, and once that occurs, no other sperm can penetrate that egg. Rapid chemical changes within the egg and the woman's body prevent another fertilization.

The combined genetic material (the DNA from the egg and sperm) carries a set of instructions, called genes, for how the egg will develop into a baby, a child, and an adult.

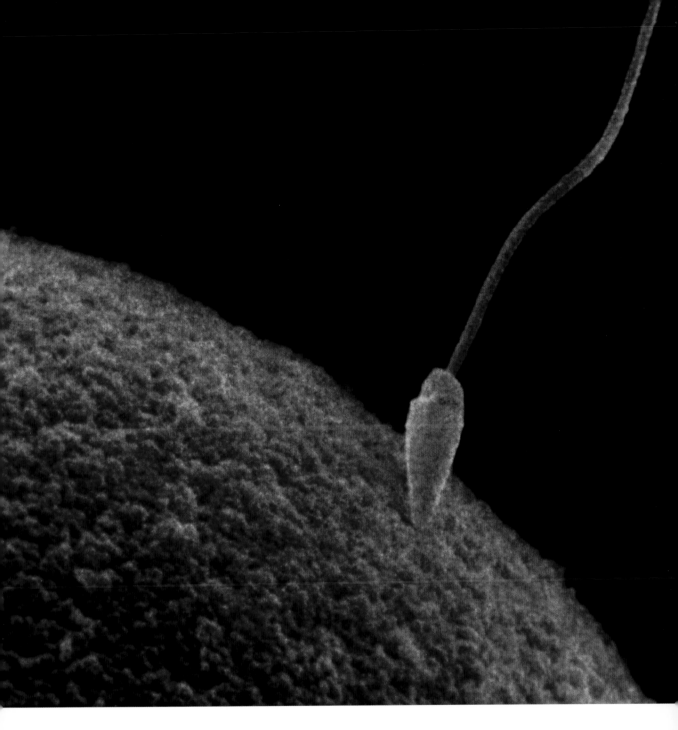

A man can usually release sperm at any time. A woman only produces a ripe egg once every twenty-eight days or so, and this egg can be fertilized for only two or three days after its release. Also, the sperm live for about two, or maybe three, days inside the female body. This is why timing the woman's cycle is important for couples who are trying to have a baby. To be successful, they need to get egg and sperm together in the right place at the right time.

An electron micrograph (a photo taken with an electron microscope) shows a human sperm fertilizing an egg. Although the man releases millions of sperm, only a few hundred find the egg, and only one of these actually fertilizes the egg.

From blastocyst to embryo

Hours after egg and sperm join, the fertilized egg divides, or splits in half, to make two cells. A few hours later, the same thing happens again, forming four cells, then eight cells, then sixteen cells, and so on. This first stage of development is called a blastocyst. It is a tiny cluster of cells that drifts slowly along the fallopian tube to the uterus.

The blastocyst's cells continue to multiply. A few days after fertilization, it contains hundreds of cells. Some of the outer cells begin to make a hormone called human chorionic gonadotropin, or

A human embryo at five weeks. At this stage, its eyes and ears have started to form, and the hands and feet have fingers and toes. It is less than one-half inch (about 10 mm) long.

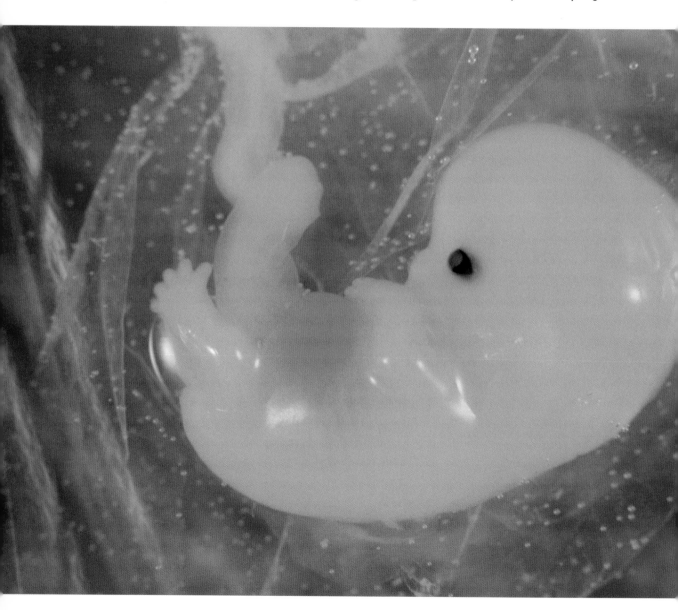

hCG. The hCG makes the corpus luteum in the ovary keep producing its hormones, estrogen and progesterone. This ensures that the uterus lining stays thick and blood-rich.

About one week after fertilization, the blastocyst implants (sinks) into the soft lining of the uterus. The lining is rich in blood and provides nourishment for the fast-multiplying cells. These cells become specialized, or "differentiate," into cells that form the brain, heart, and stomach in what is now at a stage called an embryo.

At two months after fertilization, the embryo is only about the size of a large grape. Amazingly, all of its main body parts are formed, and its heart is beating.

Fetus

From two months after fertilization until birth, the developing baby is called a fetus. It grows rapidly in size, can move about inside the uterus, and develops the finishing touches to its body, such as eyebrows, fingernails, and toenails. Finally, nine months after fertilization, the fetus is ready to leave the uterus. It passes through the uterus's neck, or cervix, and out through the vagina. As it emerges into the outside world, a baby is born.

CUTTING EDGE   FACTS

Ultrasound scanners

In the 1950s, it became possible for parents to "see" their fetus in the uterus, using the newly developed ultrasound scanner. A probe on this device sends out ultrasound waves (sound waves that are too high-pitched for human ears). When the scanner's probe is applied to a pregnant woman's abdomen, different parts of the fetus's body reflect the sound waves differently. The reflections are analyzed by computer to form an image of the fetus. By the 1980s, ultrasound scans became a routine procedure during pregnancy. Researchers also started using ultrasound scans in their fertility studies. For example, ultraound can check a woman's internal anatomy for abnormalities that might prevent her from conceiving. Abnormalities that cause infertility include misshapen fallopian tubes, missing ovaries, or abnormal growths. Improvements to ultrasound techniques continue, making it possible to see tiny details of ripe egg follicles and early embryos.

CHAPTER 2

Pioneers of IVF

Scientists have understood the exact process of human reproduction for less than one hundred years. Attempts to help people who could not have children become successful at producing a child, however, go back way before this time. About eighteen hundred years ago, in the Middle East, doctors wondered whether a woman could become pregnant if sperm containing semen was placed in her vagina artificially, rather than during normal sex. Today, we call this artificial insemination, or AI.

Gradually, the technique of AI was attempted in animals. About five hundred years ago, Arab horse breeders were using AI, and by three hundred years ago, it was being used on reptiles and dogs. AI was commonly used on farm animals throughout the last century. The first human birth by AI was in 1785, but this was an isolated case.

Increasing knowledge

Scientists made important advances in understanding the menstrual cycle in the early 1900s. In 1936, Carl Hartman of the Carnegie Institute in Baltimore, Maryland, showed that for most of the menstrual cycle, a baby could not be conceived. The most fertile time (the time when the woman is most capable of reproducing) occurs just after the ripe egg is released from the ovary (ovulation).

CUTTING EDGE MOMENTS

The first baby born by AI

The first clear report of assisted reproduction in humans using AI occurred in 1785. Scottish surgeon John Hunter examined a male patient whose urethra (the tube through the penis) was misshapen. He suggested that the man collect his semen and use a syringe to put the semen into his wife's reproductive tract. The couple had a baby later that year. Since people did not understand the timing of the menstrual cycle in 1785, the couple was very lucky. Similar attempts at AI followed in the late eighteenth and early twentieth centuries, but almost all failed.

Lazzaro Spallanzani (1729–1799) was an Italian biologist and pioneer of artificial insemination. He achieved AI in amphibians, insects, and dogs.

Hartman's work led to more attempts at human AI, with much greater success. By 1941, more than ten thousand women had conceived by AI. For some couples who wished to use AI, however, the man could not produce enough—or healthy enough—sperm. This led to the practice of AID, or artificial insemination by donor. In AID, another man, who is not the woman's partner, donates (provides) enough healthy sperm for conception (the fertilization of one of her eggs). The donor may be known to the couple or anonymous (his identity kept secret).

More and more methods

In 1949, Piero Donini discovered fertility drugs, and the first baby conceived with the help of these drugs was born in 1962. Others quickly followed. The popular term "test-tube babies" was applied to children conceived by this method. Some twenty-five years later, the same term would be used for IVF babies.

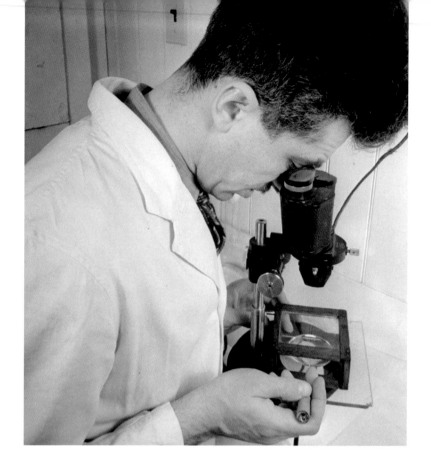

U.S. biologist Dr. Gregory Pincus (1903–1967) made headlines in 1934 by achieving IVF in rabbits. The idea of IVF shocked many people at the time, and the controversy threatened Pincus's career.

Meanwhile, in 1954, the first babies were born through AI using frozen sperm. This technique allowed batches of donated sperm to be frozen and then used later, with the identity of the donor kept secret. Gradually, doctors were expanding the types of procedures used for assisting reproduction—which now included AI, AID, AID using frozen sperm, and fertility drugs.

First external fertilization

The early methods for assisting reproduction helped large numbers of couples who previously could not conceive. The techniques did not suit others with different fertility problems, however. For example, women with blocked fallopian tubes could not be helped by AI. Doctors and medical specialists continued their research to help these patients.

In 1944, Dr. John Rock, a reproductive specialist at Harvard University in Cambridge, Massachusetts, investigated how to fertilize an egg outside the human body—the first attempts at IVF. His experiments failed, but in the 1960s, fertility researchers revisited Rock's research and the possibility of IVF. In 1969, Robert Edwards, a fertility researcher at Cambridge University in England, experimented by placing eggs in a fluid called a culture medium. It contained carefully chosen nutrients and chemicals that mimicked the conditions in the fallopian tube. Edwards successfully fertilized several eggs. He did not keep the fertilized eggs or try to grow them, so no pregnancies or babies resulted.

Obtaining eggs

In the late 1960s, at Royal Oldham Hospital in Lancashire, England, surgeon Patrick Steptoe was using a device called a laparoscope to harvest, or obtain, eggs from female patients. Steptoe used this procedure to supply eggs to fertility researchers such as Edwards. Steptoe was a gynecologist—an expert who specializes in treating females. A laparoscope is a telescope-like device that allows doctors to view the internal organs, such as the stomach or ovaries. The laparoscope is inserted through a small cut in the skin. Steptoe pioneered using the laparoscope to harvest eggs.

The birth of IVF

During the early 1970s, Steptoe and Edwards began to work together to develop IVF. At that time, they did not use fertility drugs on their patients. Instead, they monitored the patients very carefully, twenty-four hours a day, and used the laparoscope to remove the just-released ripe eggs. Steptoe and Edwards also worked to make the culture media more natural. Eggs and sperm that felt more "at home" would survive longer in the culture dishes and have more of a chance of becoming early embryos.

CUTTING EDGE MOMENTS

Landmark experiments with animals

Before attempting AI and IVF on humans, researchers experimented with these techniques on animals. Many of the techniques have since become routine methods for breeding livestock on farms.

- In 1949, chicken sperm was successfully frozen and thawed.
- In 1951, an embryo was transferred from one cow to another.
- In 1952, the first cow was born through AI using frozen sperm.
- In 1959, the first mammal, a rabbit, was born by IVF.
- In 1972, baby mice were born after being frozen as embryos.

In 1973, an IVF pregnancy began in the United States, but it was stopped very early amid much controversy, leading to a complex legal battle (*see page 51*). In 1975, an IVF attempt by Edwards and Steptoe ended when the embryo failed to grow.

Success

As news of IVF research leaked out, it sparked a fierce public debate. Many people felt that human reproduction should be left to nature and God's will. Despite the controversy surrounding their work, Edwards and Steptoe continued. One of their patients was Lesley Brown, who had been trying for a baby with her husband John for nine years, without success. In 1977, one of her ripe eggs

Louise Brown, the world's first test-tube baby, shortly after her birth at Oldham General Hospital, Lancashire, England.

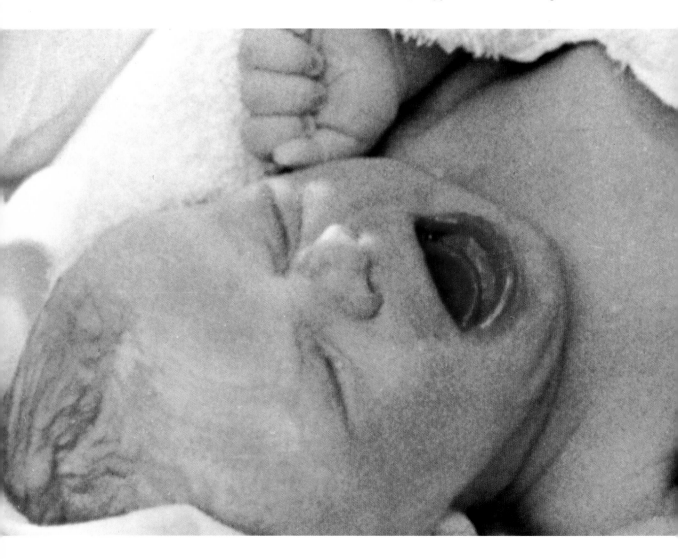

was removed, fertilized with John's sperm, and replaced in her uterus. Nine months later, Lesley gave birth to a healthy baby girl, Louise Brown. Louise was the first IVF baby, and Steptoe and Edwards were present at her birth. Four years later, Lesley and John had another daughter, Natalie—also by IVF.

News of the birth of Louise Brown shook the world. As a new type of fertility treatment, it gave hope to millions of couples who wanted children but could not conceive. The event also provoked storms of protest from a variety of people, especially from some religious leaders, who not only regarded infertility (the inability to reproduce) as a condition that God intended for some couples, but also viewed IVF as an example of meddling with "God's will."

IVF takes off

Soon, research teams in other countries attempted IVF, and the number of IVF births accelerated. IVF performed at clinics in Melbourne, Australia, resulted in twelve of the first fifteen IVF babies born there. Australia has been at the cutting edge of IVF research ever since. Elizabeth Carr, born in Norfolk, Virginia, on December 28, 1981, was the first "test-tube baby" born in the U.S.

The Norfolk IVF clinic was the first such clinic in the United States. It opened in 1980 in the face of great opposition from anti-abortion protestors. (Abortion is the removal of an embryo or fetus from the uterus in order to end a pregnancy.) Over the years, most of the opposition faded. Today, IVF is an established medical procedure—and just one type of ART (*see page 6*).

CUTTING EDGE MOMENTS

The first IVF baby

Louise Brown, the world's first IVF baby, was born on July 25, 1978. Her birth had a huge global impact. People were relieved that Louise was healthy and normal. Today, she lives in Bristol, England, and works for the postal service. In October 2003, along with many others conceived using IVF, she celebrated her twenty-fifth birthday. In 2004, she married Wesley Mullinder. Dr. Robert Edwards was guest of honor at the wedding. Louise is now pregnant. Her expected delivery date is January 2007.

CHAPTER 3

When and How IVF Is Done

IVF is usually recommended as one of several options for couples who are unable to conceive a baby through natural means. Before couples attempt IVF, however, they must know if it is the right treatment option.

Couples considered for IVF must have been unsuccessfully trying to conceive a baby for at least two years. Their family doctor or fertility specialist should inform them about the best chances of reproduction. Couples must also understand the importance of timing sex and the release of the egg (ovulation)—indicated by a slight rise in the woman's "basal" body temperature. They need to plot those temperatures on a chart to pinpoint the day of ovulation. Special kits that measure the hormone levels in urine and indicate when ovulation occurs are also available.

If, after following these basic routines for a few months, pregnancy still does not occur, the doctor will perform a few tests to determine whether there is a medical problem with the woman, the man, or both.

The doctor may test the couple for signs of a medical condition that may have caused one or both to become infertile (unable to reproduce). Problems might include a previous

CUTTING EDGE — FACTS

Surveys of fertility problems

Recent surveys in countries that carry out IVF regularly show that overall:

- About 10 to 20 percent of couples have problems conceiving a baby. (Although these couples are sometimes considered infertile, ART can help many of them become parents.)
- About one-third to two-fifths of these cases involve problems with the male and are known as male factor infertility.
- A similar number involve problems with the female and are known as female factor infertility.
- In 10 to 25 percent of cases, problems are found with both the female and male.
- In about one-tenth of the remaining cases, the exact problem cannot be found. These are known medically as idiopathic (no identifiable cause) cases, but even so, IVF is sometimes successful.

injury or infection of the reproductive parts. In some cases, a psychological (mind-related) difficulty—such as depression—suffered by either the man or the woman can be the main stumbling block to conceiving a baby.

Fertility checks

Depending on the results of these early checks and examinations, the couple usually participates in some meetings with fertility counselors at a hospital or clinic. Many times, the doctor orders further tests to find the cause of the problem.

A couple consults with a fertility specialist. Doctors seek to establish the cause of infertility before deciding whether to proceed with IVF or some other form of assisted reproduction.

These specialized tests include checking the hormone levels of both partners. Low hormone levels in a female may prevent her eggs from ripening or prevent ovulation. Low hormone levels in the male may prevent proper sperm formation.

Medical staff also check for evidence of infections or abnormalities, which may have caused swelling or the formation of scar tissue that blocks the tubes that carry eggs or sperm.

Doctors observe the semen under a microscope to perform a sperm count (a test for the normal number of sperm per amount of seminal fluid). If fewer than normal numbers of sperm are seen, the man is considered to have a low sperm count (*see pages 24–25*), which makes conception by the natural method unlikely.

CUTTING EDGE — FACTS

Allergy to sperm

In some cases, a couple's inability to conceive may not be a lack of fertility. The woman may develop a condition similar to an allergy, in which her body reacts against her partner's sperm. Doctors can identify this allergy by finding substances called sperm antibodies in her blood. (Antibodies are substances produced by the body to help protect it from disease.) In such cases, the best solution might be to use donated sperm from another man.

Female infertility

Female infertility has many causes. Some women become infertile because of a problem with their fallopian tubes (oviducts) that prevents eggs and sperm from passing through or surviving within them. Tubal problems may be caused by abnormal development when the woman was young, causing the tubes to be absent or malformed. The tubes may be scarred, twisted, or blocked due to infection, injury, a previous operation, or an ectopic pregnancy. An ectopic pregnancy occurs when the fertilized egg implants and begins developing within the fallopian tube instead of within the uterus. It damages the tube. Treatment usually requires surgery.

An infection of the fallopian tubes, sometimes caused by pelvic inflammatory disease (PID), commonly results in tubal obstruction. In certain cases, surgery can repair the tube so that eggs can pass, but IVF is another option. Tubal problems affect about one-third of the women who cannot conceive in the usual way.

Endometriosis is a disease of the female reproductive system in which patches or lumps resembling the endometrium (the lining of the uterus) migrate (move) to other parts of the abdominal area. The patches thicken and bleed with the menstrual cycle, just like the uterus lining. About one-third of the women who suffer from endometriosis have difficulty conceiving. The disease also increases the risk of an ectopic pregnancy.

Women may also suffer from other conditions that can cause infertility. Some women develop uterine fibroids, which are lumps or growths in the uterus, either on the outside or inside of its muscular wall, or within the wall's thickness.

They may also have polyps—smaller growths the size and shape of grapes, usually on the lining of the uterus's neck, the cervix. Ovarian cysts present another problem that can cause problems with conception. Many of these conditions require surgery.

This color X-ray shows a blockage and swelling of the left fallopian tube (on the right in the photo) near the uterus (the central triangular object).

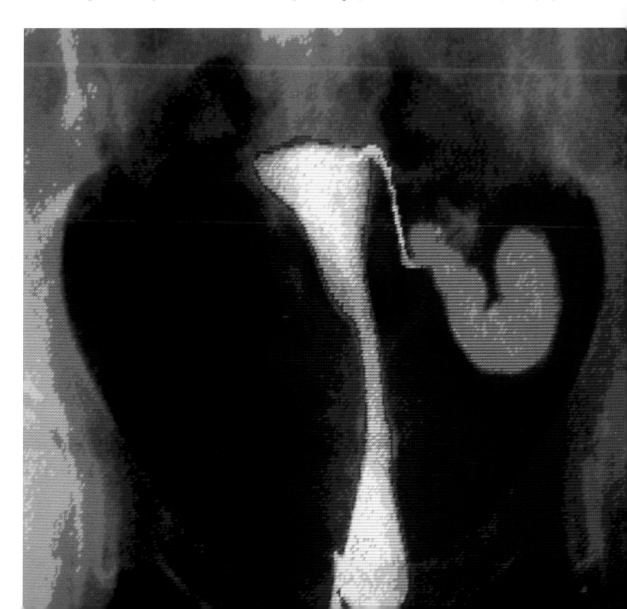

Uterine fibroids and polyps affect the conditions and balance of natural chemicals within the uterus, making it difficult for sperm to pass through or for a blastocyst to implant there. Women may have one or more ovarian cysts—fluid-filled bags or sacs that grow within the ovary (sometimes to very large sizes) and disrupt the ovary's production of female hormones.

In rare cases, a woman may have no ovaries, or the ovaries lack eggs. In these cases, IVF may still be possible using donated eggs. IVF has also helped postmenopausal women (women who have reached the age when they have stopped menstruating) to become mothers (*see page 36–37*).

Male infertility

As with women, there is a range of reasons for infertility in men. These reasons are collectively known as male factor infertility. In some men, the testicles produce no sperm, even though the rest of the reproductive organs work well, look normal, and produce seminal fluid. Sometimes, a large proportion of the sperm may be malformed: They lack tails, have two heads, or a "kinked neck." They may swim around in circles instead of in a straight line.

Some men do not produce enough sperm. This condition is called oligospermia. A man with a sperm count of less than twenty million sperm per 0.03 ounce (1 ml) of semen has a low sperm count. Several factors can affect sperm production. Smoking, drinking alcohol, taking drugs, catching an infection such as mumps, and high levels of stress and anxiety can all cause a lowering of the sperm count. Even wearing underwear that is too tight can cause this condition.

CUTTING EDGE SCIENCE

Sperm production and obesity

A medical study in 2005 showed clearly for the first time that obesity affects sperm production. The more obese the male, the more likely his sperm will have "fragmented DNA"—the genetic material (DNA) inside these sperm is broken or in pieces. Sperm with fragmented DNA are less likely to fertilize an egg, and—if they do—the embryo runs a higher risk of malformation.

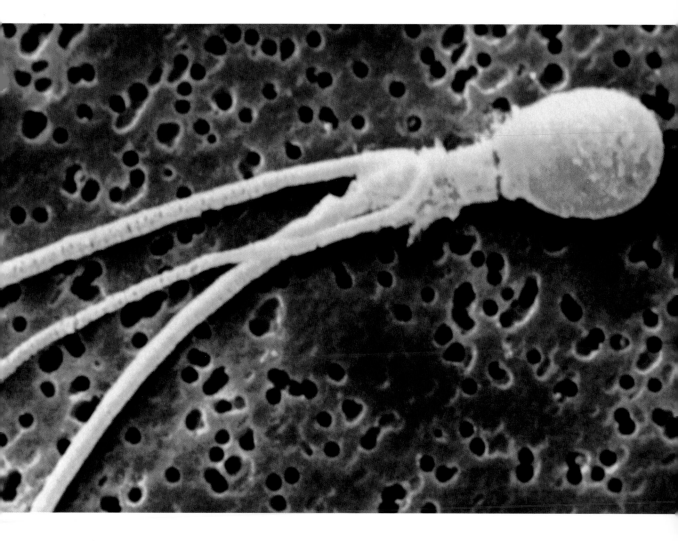

The testicles must be kept slightly cooler than the main body temperature for optimum sperm production. Tight underwear holds the organs too close to the lower abdomen, which causes them to become too warm.

A lack or imbalance of male hormones, exposure to some kinds of radiation or toxic substances, such as lead or mercury, and certain medications, such as drugs used against cancer, can also cause a reduction in sperm production.

Sometimes, the tubes that the sperm travel through may be absent or malformed. Tubal scarring or blocking results from an injury, a previous operation, an infection, such as cystitis, or a sexually transmitted disease (a disease, such as gonorrhea, that is passed from one person to another during sexual contact).

This sperm has three tails instead of the usual one. Deformed sperm can lead to male infertility. In this case, the sperm's mobility may be hindered by having several tails. There are many possible causes of deformed sperm, including blockages in the sperm tubes or sexually transmitted diseases.

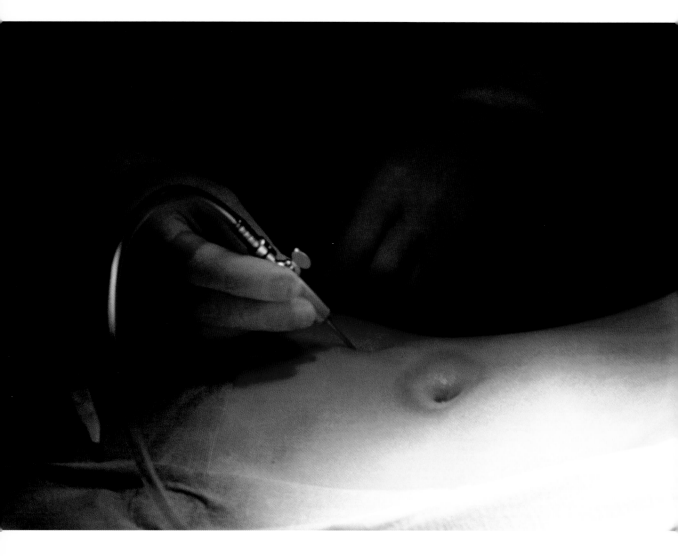

Is IVF the right solution?

When the infertility problem has been diagnosed (identified), the couple and their doctor can discuss suitable treatment. This may be fertility drugs, AI (artificial insemination), IVF, or perhaps a different solution, such as adoption.

Once the couple and their doctor have agreed that IVF is the best solution, the doctor explains the process to them in detail. The procedures, risks, and chances for success are clearly outlined. (*See Chapter 5 for more information about the risks and chances for success.*) Before any procedures are attempted, the informed couple must sign various "consent" forms that explain what doctors will do, the possible results, and what, if any, side effects to expect.

A surgeon inserts an instrument called a laparoscope into a woman's abdomen to obtain her eggs. The laparoscope is linked to a video camera so the surgeon can see the ovaries.

Their doctor may recommend psychological counseling. These experts assess how well the couple will cope with the stresses involved in IVF—especially when an in vitro attempt fails.

The stages of IVF

Standard IVF treatment has four main stages. These are:

- Obtaining the eggs
- Obtaining the sperm
- The fertilization process and related procedures that control embryonic development
- Placing the early-stage embryo inside the woman's uterus

Obtaining the eggs Depending on the woman's condition, she may or may not be producing ripe eggs naturally. The ripe egg follicle is visible on a detailed vaginal ultrasound scan if the probe is placed inside the vagina near the ovaries. The woman's progress through her menstrual cycle can also be followed using a temperature chart and blood tests for checking hormone levels so doctors can predict the release of a ripe egg.

When the egg is ripe and ready for release, the doctor uses a needle—placed through the vaginal wall and guided by an ultrasound image—to "suck up," or aspirate, the egg and its fluid into the needle. The doctor then checks the fluid under a microscope to verify that an egg is present.

CUTTING EDGE   SCIENCE

Making eggs and sperm from body cells

Since the mid-1990s, researchers have tried to make egg and sperm cells from the types of unspecialized cells known as stem cells (*see page 49*). Animal experiments show that if certain kinds of stem cells are placed together and "fed" a particular mix of chemicals, they clump into groups similar to ovarian follicles. Gradually, one cell grows larger and undergoes the special type of cell division that produces an egg. In 2005, similar experiments used an animal's ordinary body cells instead of stem cells. This research suggests that one day it may be possible to help people who cannot produce eggs or sperm become parents by producing egg and sperm cells from their own body cells.

A technician uses a pipette and a microscope to prepare a human egg cell for IVF. The outer layer of cells, called the corona radiata, is being removed from the egg to encourage fertilization.

Each course of IVF treatment is carefully tailored to the individual woman, the timing of her fertility cycle, and her particular hormone levels. In general, most women receive a series of artificial hormones and drugs designed to produce several ripe eggs in the best condition, at the best time, for the greatest chance of fertlization.

Some of the hormones and drugs are given by injection, others as a nasal spray or tablets. The number and timing of doses is determined by the medical team. Most fertility treatments involve taking drugs every day or two.

The treatment goal is to make several eggs (up to a dozen) ripen at the same time, a condition called super-ovulation. The technique of having several eggs to mix with sperm gives more chance of at least one embryo forming after fertilization. Also, the hormonal and drug treatments may have side effects (*see page 44*). So, if several eggs are obtained from one cycle, these can be used for more than one attempt at IVF (should the first one fail), and the woman has to undergo only one session of hormonal and drug treatment.

During this time, the woman's menstrual cycle is monitored by blood tests and body temperature readings. As the expected time of egg release approaches, she may receive a "trigger" injection. This contains a hormone that triggers or causes release of the eggs at a fairly exact time, usually thiry-six hours after the injection.

Precisely timing the egg release allows the woman and her medical team to plan for collecting the eggs. This step is an improvement on earlier forms of IVF (before the use of trigger injections), when eggs might be released at almost any time, including the middle of the night.

Obtaining the sperm No surgery or drugs are normally required for obtaining a sperm sample. Sometimes, however, the vas deferens (sperm tubes) are blocked because of a previous injury or infection. In such cases, there are a number of methods, known collectively as surgical sperm collection (SSC).

For example, sperm can be obtained from the epididymides, the coiled tube next to the testicle where the sperm are stored. The doctor makes small cuts in the scrotum and epididymides, and the sperm are gently squeezed out or aspirated through a needle.

CUTTING EDGE MOMENTS

IVF firsts

After the birth of Louise Brown, many other IVF firsts followed:

- **1982** The first test-tube twins were born in England to parents Jo and Stewart Smith. (The tendency today is to avoid multiple births because it increases the risk of complications—*see page 42*.)
- **1983** In Australia, the first baby was born from a frozen embryo that was thawed and transferred to the uterus.
- **1984** A woman in Australia with no ovaries gave birth using IVF, donor eggs, and hormone treatments.

Once the sperm are obtained, the IVF team must capacitate them. Capacitation is a process that naturally happens to sperm after they enter the woman's body. The front end, or "cap," of the sperm changes in consistency to make it ready to join with the egg when it makes contact, and the sperm's outer membrane also alters, becoming more flexible, so the sperm can swim more effectively. Capacitation makes fertilization of the egg much more likely. The IVF team mimics the conditions naturally experienced by the sperm by adding various chemicals to the culture fluid and carefully controlling the temperature. This process artificially capacitates the sperm.

CUTTING EDGE　　　　**FACTS**

IVF statistics
- Between 1978 (first successful use of IVF), and 2005, almost two million babies around the world were born using IVF and similar ARTs (assisted reproductive technologies).
- In the United States and England, about one baby in one hundred is conceived using IVF or ARTs.
- In Australia, the proportion of all births using IVF or ARTs is one baby in fifty.
- In Iceland, the number of births due to IVF or ARTs is about one in twenty-five babies.

Mixing eggs and sperm The eggs and sperm are examined under a microscope and the healthiest ones are selected. Then, the eggs and sperm are placed in a dish that contains a carefully controlled mix of the right temperature, hormones, and other chemicals, that are found under natural conditions in the female reproductive tract. The following day, the mixture is checked again under a microscope for fertilized eggs (which are often also called embryos). Any that appear ready are prepared for placement in the woman's uterus.

Before placement in the woman's uterus, however, one or two cells from each embryo may be removed and tested. The goal at this stage is to detect and discard cells containing faulty genes that may cause genetic (inherited) diseases, such as cystic fibrosis. This testing process is called preimplantation genetic diagnosis (PGD). (*For more details about PGD, see pages 56 to 57.*)

In many cases, unused embryos are frozen in case of failed transfer attempts. Sometimes, spare embryos are used for stem cell research (*see page 49*)—although this practice is controversial and illegal in many countries. The United States does not allow the use of federal monies for such research, but private U.S. companies can do so. Frozen embryos are also stored for future, unknown uses.

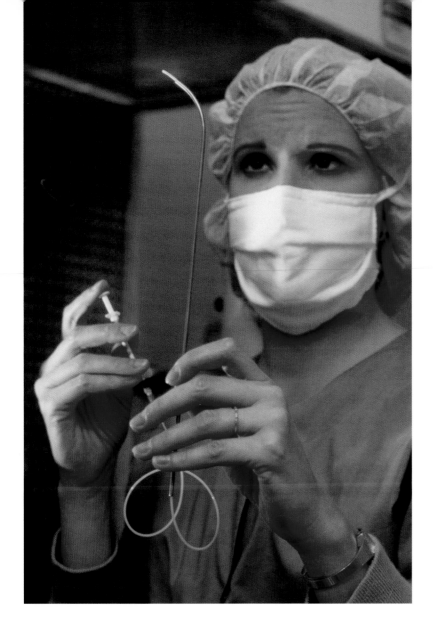

A technician holds a catheter containing several embryos that are ready to be transferred into the mother's uterus.

Into the uterus The fourth and final stage of IVF is embryo transfer —the placing of the embryo in the mother's uterus. This is done through a narrow tube called a catheter that is passed through the vagina and cervix into the uterus.

After the embryo has been transferred, the woman may be given further hormone injections and perhaps pessaries (tablets containing hormones that must be placed in the vagina) to help the embryo implant itself in the lining of the uterus. Blood tests are often used to check that the embryo is implanted and the pregnancy is established. Another ultrasound scan is usually taken to check the progress of the procedure. At this stage, the woman is considered successfully pregnant, and IVF is complete.

Variations on IVF

There are many variations on the standard pattern of IVF, with each couple receiving treatment tailored to their particular requirements.

ICSI An increasingly common variation of IVF is intracytoplasmic sperm injection, or ICSI. In this technique, instead of allowing sperm and eggs to mingle freely, a single sperm is injected directly into an egg, using a microneedle (a very tiny, hollow needle attached to a syringe). ICSI can be a useful method if the man's sperm count is low and is especially useful if many abnormal sperm are present. A healthy-looking individual sperm is selected and taken into a microneedle. The needle's tip is pushed through the outer wall of the egg, and the sperm is injected into the egg's interior.

CUTTING EDGE   SCIENCE

ICSI breakthrough?

Researchers are continually trying to improve methods such as ICSI. In 2005, researchers working on mouse sperm at the University of Hawaii School of Medicine showed that breaking the sperm's "cap" (the acrosome) at the front end of the sperm may increase the chances of successful fertilization when using ICSI. The acrosome usually pushes against the egg and forms an opening so that the sperm's DNA passes into the mouse egg. Further tests may show whether this also happens in humans.

Assisted hatching Another variation on IVF is called assisted hatching, or laser hatching. This technique is usually carried out in cases where, for various reasons (which are sometimes never discovered), previous attempts at IVF have failed at the implantation stage. A laser beam or chemical makes a small hole in the outer shell of the early embryo before it is placed into the uterus. This gives the embryo a better chance of implanting in the uterine wall.

GIFT, ZIFT, and TET In some cases, inserting the embryo into the uterus through the cervix is difficult because of, for instance, a very narrow or abnormally shaped cervix, which makes standard IVF problematic. In these cases, doctors may choose to use one of the following techniques.

GIFT stands for gamete intrafallopian tube transfer. In this technique, eggs and sperm (which are known as gametes) are collected and checked as in a standard IVF procedure. But instead of placing the eggs and sperm into a culture medium, they are put back into the woman's fallopian tube using a laparoscope. Fertilization then takes place in the fallopian tube, as happens in natural conceptions.

ZIFT stands for zygote intrafallopian transfer. The procedure resembles the standard pattern of IVF, with eggs fertilized in a culture medium. With ZIFT, however, the fertilized egg (which is technically called a zygote) is put into the woman's fallopian tube instead of her uterus.

TET, which stands for tubal embryo transfer, is similar to ZIFT but more delayed. The fertilized egg is allowed to develop into an early embryo before being put in the fallopian tube.

Some fertility centers and clinics use these variations on IVF when appropriate. Standard IVF and IVF using ICSI are generally the most common and effective techniques.

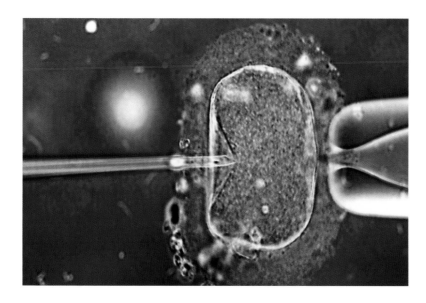

This micrograph shows the IVF technique known as ICSI: A human egg is about to be pierced by a microneedle containing a single sperm.

CHAPTER 4

Family Matters

In the early days of IVF, couples were interviewed to make sure they were in a stable, long-term relationship—and preferably married. Over the years, social attitudes have become more relaxed in many countries. At the same time, advances in IVF have expanded the range of people who can bear children. Today, many people for whom childbearing may previously have been impossible are using IVF to have children. These include older women, same-sex couples, and even women who wish to have a child using their dead husband's sperm.

CUTTING EDGE — DEBATES

Who should receive IVF?

The overriding goal of the medical teams responsible for carrying out IVF is that the process is successful and that the baby is born healthy. Some people question to what extent these teams should concern themselves with the well-being of those they help to bring into the world. For example, should IVF be offered to a couple with a high risk of inherited disease, or to a couple who smoke heavily, drink to excess and abuse drugs? None of these people, if naturally fertile, would be prevented by law from having a baby in the usual way. Should they be barred from having a child by using IVF if they have the money to pay for the treatment?

Children for same-sex couples

Advances in IVF are creating more options and new situations. It is now possible for a same-sex female couple to use the eggs from one of the women and donated sperm to have a baby. A same-sex male

couple can use the sperm from one of the men, a donated egg, and a woman, known as a surrogate, to have a baby (*see page 37*). By making such situations possible, IVF has helped challenge traditional views about what constitutes a family.

A same-sex male couple holds their two-month-old adopted daughter. Today, IVF offers same-sex couples the chance to have and raise a child that is biologically related to one of the partners.

Savior siblings

A child with a serious disease might be helped by a transplant of, for example, bone marrow. Rejection is a problem with all transplants, however. The body's immune system may identify the transplant material as "foreign" and attack ("reject") it. Rejection is much less likely, though, if the transplanted tissue or ogran has the same blood and tissue type as that of the recipient. Parents of children with serious diseases, who might be helped by a transplant, are often tempted to have another child who could provide transplant material for the child with problems. Transplant tissues from a sibling are less likely to be rejected because of the close genetic relationship between brothers and sisters.

If the disease is inherited, however, the younger sibling might inherit it, too. An IVF technique known as pre-implantation genetic diagnosis (PGD) offers a solution (*see pages 56–57*). With PGD, one—or sometimes two—cells from an early embryo can be genetically tested. Doctors can then use PGD to check whether the embryo will grow into a child with the potential for the disease. Using this technique, the couple can be much more certain that their second child will be healthy and also able to help their older, sick child.

Too old to have a baby?

Most women reach the end of their natural fertile life between the ages of about fifty and fifty-five. This biological state is called

Adriana Iliescu, aged sixty-seven, with her one-year-old daughter, Eliza Maria. Some people do not think it is "right" for a woman of that age to produce a child. Other people argue that as long as both mother and child are healthy and happy, it is no one else's business.

CUTTING EDGE MOMENTS

Oldest IVF mother

In January 2005, retired Romanian professor Adriana became the world's oldest mother. At age sixty-six, she gave birth to a daughter using IVF. During a previous IVF attempt, Iliescu was pregnant with twins, but one twin miscarried and the other was stillborn. Her case highlights the risks for older mothers. Opponents to IVF for older women point out that when Iliescu's daughter celebrates her twenty-first birthday, Iliescu will be eighty-seven. Other people see no problem with older parents having children.

menopause, when the regular female cycle becomes erratic and then fades away. Hormone balance changes, and eggs no longer ripen. It is not possible to have a baby by natural means.

IVF and hormone treatments have made it possible for many women over fifty, and some older than sixty, to give birth using donated eggs. A recent survey showed that post-menopausal women may experience more complications in pregnancy, such as high blood pressure. Apart from that, however, the chances of having a healthy baby, or of a miscarriage, are not much different from those of younger women.

So it is now medically possible for older women to have babies, but what about the family and social implications? When the baby becomes a teenager, the mother may be in her seventies, which may present difficulties for both parent and child. Similar arguments apply as well when a man over fifty becomes a father.

Who are the parents?

IVF offers people a number of choices about how they conceive and bear children. This can sometimes cause confusion and occasionally legal disputes about who the child's "real" parents are. For example, IVF allows various alternatives to a woman using her own eggs. These include eggs donated by a relative or friend, or eggs obtained from a donor "bank."

Similarly, a woman does not have to use her own uterus. Through the use of IVF, an early embryo can be placed into the uterus of another woman—known as a surrogate mother. The surrogate carries the baby until birth and gives it up.

As with eggs, sperm can come from either the partner or from an anonymous donor, a friend, or family member. The sperm may be frozen, and, like eggs, can be obtained from a sperm bank, a fertility clinic, or through an Internet contact. Sperm cells can be frozen and then thawed. They are good for many years.

These choices make it possible for a child born through IVF to have several mothers and fathers. A baby may be conceived using eggs from one woman, the egg donor, who is the biological, or

An IVF technician freezes samples of sperm and eggs in order to store them. Eggs and sperm can be kept at about -292˚ Fahrenheit (-180˚ Celsius) for long periods and then returned to normal temperature without causing them any damage.

natural, mother; the fetus may develop in the uterus of another woman, the surrogate mother; and then be cared for and raised by a third woman—the one the child recognizes as its "real" mother.

Similarly, there can be a both a biological father (known or unknown, depending from where the sperm came) and a father who raises the child and is regarded as the "real" father. Or, there may only be a biological father, for example, in the case of families with a single mother.

Frozen eggs and sperm

Many IVF centers routinely freeze eggs, sperm, and embryos for possible future use. For example, a woman may learn she has a disease that will affect her ability to reproduce. She might therefore decide to have her eggs or ovary tissue removed and frozen so that she can attempt to conceive later through IVF. Alternatively, she could donate or sell the eggs. For similar reasons, a man can freeze some of his sperm.

In some cases, a woman or man may hope to use the frozen eggs or sperm of a former partner in order to conceive a baby by IVF. Many legal questions arise from this situation. If the partners are divorced, who "owns" these frozen eggs or sperm if there is no legal agreement signed by both? If two unmarried partners had eggs and sperm frozen, but then end their relationship, does either ex-partner retain the right to use the other's genetic material? Such situations are regularly tested in courts.

CUTTING EDGE   MOMENTS

Diane Blood

Briton Stephen Blood contracted meningitis in 1995, slipped into a coma, and then died. While he was comatose, a sample of his sperm was frozen. His widow, Diane, wished to use Stephen's frozen sperm to have a child through IVF. England's Human Fertilization and Embryology Authority (HFEA) refused the widow permission to use the sperm because Stephen had never given written permission. Diane went to Belgium, had IVF treatment with Stephen's sperm there, and gave birth to a boy in 1998. After that, England's Court of Appeal reversed the HFEA's ruling. Mrs. Blood also gave birth to a second son conceived through IVF using her dead husband's sperm.

CHAPTER 5

Success, Risk, and Failure

For most people, success in IVF means the birth of a baby. By this definition, the success rate of IVF is about 20 to 25 percent worldwide. In other words, only one in four or five attempts at IVF (known as IVF cycles) lead to the birth of a baby. Many women improve their own individual chances of having a baby by having repeated IVF cycles.

It is interesting to note, however, that the chances of a couple conceiving naturally during each menstrual cycle are also about one in five. When viewed this way, IVF is roughly as successful as natural attempts at conception. In fact, by all indications, the long-term success rate of IVF steadily increases annually.

Varied success

The success rates of IVF are affected by a number of factors. Older women, for example, are less likely to have successful attempts. Studies in 2004 and 2005 show that the average chances of IVF success for women under age thirty-five run higher than 40 percent, while for those over forty years, the success rate is less than 5 percent. Success rates are also lower for women who smoke or are overweight. A 2005 survey in the Netherlands showed that being overweight reduced the chances of IVF success by as much as one-third.

CUTTING EDGE — FACTS

The effects of smoking

In 2005, a large survey carried out in the Netherlands showed that smoking cigarettes has a "devastating impact" on a woman's chances of having a baby using IVF. The survey included more than eight thousand women aged twenty to forty-five. On average, smoking more than one cigarette a day for one year reduced the likelihood of having a baby by IVF by between one-quarter and one-third. Scientists believe that the toxic (poisonous) chemicals in tobacco smoke may affect the lining of the uterus or harm the casing (known as the zona pellucida) around the ripe egg.

Other factors affecting IVF success include whether the eggs are the woman's or donated (donated eggs make IVF success less likely on average), whether they are fresh or frozen (frozen eggs reduce the chances of pregnancy—although with improving methods this is likely to change), and the reason behind the fertility problem.

Overweight women who smoke are stastistically far less likely to conceive through IVF.

IVF success also sometimes depends on where it is carried out. The success rate at some IVF clinics is high—perhaps more than 50 percent. A high success rate at a clinic is often influenced by the rules of that clinic. For instance, clinics that only accept young and otherwise healthy women for treatment will enjoy a higher success rate than clinics for "at risk" women.

Some clinics work with more difficult cases. Either partner may experience fertility problems, or they might both be above forty years of age. In these cases, individual success is less common but all the more noteworthy when it occurs.

More than one baby

As part of the IVF procedure, it is common to put two or even three early embryos into the uterus. This is called multiple embryo transfer, or MET. Experts believe MET allows more chance of an embryo implanting and growing. MET often results in a multiple pregnancy, when more than one embryo develops, which leads to the birth of twins or triplets. Multiple pregnancies always present more risks than single pregnancies, regardless of method of conception. Risks for multiple pregnances include low birth weight, premature birth, or birth defects. The higher chance for multiple pregnances and the accompanying problems makes IVF pregnancies more risky than natural pregnances.

There is a growing trend among IVF practitioners toward single embryo transfer, or SET—putting just one IVF early embryo into the

CUTTING EDGE   DEBATES

SET versus MET

A European report in 2005 compared about five hundred babies. Half were born through IVF using SET and half were conceived naturally. All parents shared similar socioeconomic and ethic backgrounds. The report found almost no differences in birth weight or incidence of premature birth. Another 2005 report compared SET babies with MET babies. It showed that MET babies were more likely to have a low birth or be delivered prematurely—even when only one MET baby was born. Often, the other embryo or fetus died in utero (inside the uterus)—an event known as the "vanishing twin." Many fertility experts now advise using SET procedures for IVF treatments instead of MET procedures.

uterus. Some countries, including Denmark and Belgium, are considering making SET a legal requirement. Spare embryos from the IVF session are frozen, and if the first IVF cycle is not successful, a second embryo is thawed and tried in a second IVF cycle, and so on. Sometimes the embryos are kept longer, perhaps for another child in the future, or even as part of stem cell research (*see page 49*).

These fraternal triplets were born through IVF. With MET, several embryos are transferred into the woman's uterus in the hope that at least one implants and develops into a baby. In this case, three of the embryos developed.

Risks to the mother

IVF poses slightly more risks to women than those who conceive naturally. Risks include allergic reaction to certain drugs, headaches, mood swings, hot flushes, vaginal dryness, ovarian cysts, ectopic pregnancy, and ovarian cancer. The latest advances in IVF treatment have helped reduce such risks.

Ovarian hyperstimulation syndrome (OHSS) is one of the potential disorders caused by IVF treatment. Symptoms vary according to which of the powerful fertility drugs are used during the treatment—especially those that make eggs ripen. About one-tenth of all women undergoing IVF are affected by OHSS. The women may experience bloating, nausea and vomiting, diarrhea, thirst, dry skin and hair, and weight gain. In more serious cases, OHSS can cause shortness of breath, blood clots in the arteries and veins, pain in the chest and lower abdomen, and abnormally enlarged ovaries, which could rupture or twist. Treatment for the latter usually involves emergency surgery.

Are IVF babies healthy?

Like all babies, a newborn IVF child is weighed in the delivery room, and his or her reflexes are tested. A quick physical exam reveals developmental problems, such as cleft palate or spina bifida. Follow-up office visits include monitoring weight and documenting milestones such as smiling, sitting up, and crawling.

CUTTING EDGE   SCIENCE

ICSI study

A long-term Belgian study of children conceived using the ICSI method of IVF (injecting a sperm into the egg) was published in 2005. The study compared about three hundred eight-year-olds. One hundred fifty of them were conceived by the ICSI method and one hundred fifty of them were conceived normally. All of the children had similar backgrounds. Studies revealed very few differences in intelligence and motor skills (movement and muscle coordination) between the groups. In fact, the ICSI group scored very slightly higher on intelligence tests. This may be because they received more attention and stimulation from parents who tried harder to conceive a baby.

Doctors can monitor children's health by checking their growth rate. The most recent surveys indicate that there is no difference between the health and development of IVF babies and those conceived naturally.

Research has shown that, overall, babies conceived by IVF had slightly higher proportions of these problems—for example, low birth weight. Each year, however, the health differences between babies born by IVF and through natural conception lessen.

In fact, a major worldwide survey in 2004 tracked IVF babies from childhood to adulthood. It showed that, on average, IVF babies were as healthy as those conceived naturally.

CHAPTER 6

Applications of IVF

The techniques developed for IVF have applications beyond helping people reproduce. For example, the fertility drug treatments used in IVF can also be used to treat other female hormone disorders that have nothing to do with reproduction. Sperm, eggs, early embryos, and methods used in IVF are also useful in many different areas of research, as the following paragraphs show.

An electron micrograph of a human X (center) and Y (lower right) sex chromosome. The sex chromosomes passed on during fertilization determine gender.

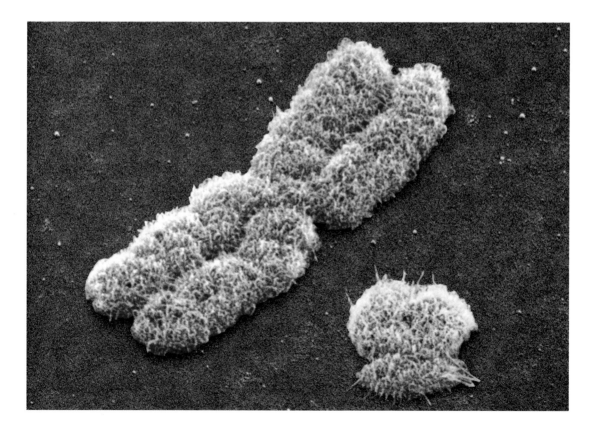

Girl or boy—you choose?

In theory, it is possible to choose the sex of an IVF baby. People might wish to do this for many reasons. Some parents may want a balance of boys and girls in the family. In some cultures, parents may prefer to have boys because a girl could prove a financial burden. In traditional societies, women must often provide a dowry (money or property) when they marry, and women have little power to earn their own money or inherit property.

Selecting the baby's sex for cultural reasons or for "family balancing" is banned in some countries, although sex selection may be allowed for medical reasons, such as to avoid inherited diseases that only affect one sex (the blood clotting disease called hemophilia, for instance, affects males almost exclusively).

IVF with ICSI makes sex selection possible. Doctors choose the sperm for injection into the egg. Genetic material in a sperm or egg is contained in twenty-three structures called chromosomes. An egg's sex chromosome always carries an X. A sperm's sex chromosome carries either an X or a Y. Injecting an X or Y sperm into the egg determines the baby's sex. So, if a sperm contains an X chromosome, the baby will be a girl (XX); if it contains a Y chromosome, the baby will be a boy (XY). Methods for separating X and Y sperm are currently being researched.

An alternative method of sex selection is to allow several eggs to be fertilized as part of the standard IVF procedure and to test the early embryos for their gender as part of PGD (*see pages 56–57*). Then, the doctor selects either a male or female embryo to put into the uterus, depending on if the parents want a girl or a boy.

CUTTING EDGE SCIENCE

Sorting X from Y

One of the methods used for determining the sex of a sperm is called flow cytometry. A special dye is added to the sperm sample. The dye colors or stains the DNA (genetic material) in the sperm. A sperm that carries a Y chromosome, which will produce a boy, stains more lightly than a sperm that carries an X chromosome. The laser inside the flow cytometer detects the difference in staining and sorts the sperm into male and female batches. The accuracy of guaranteeing a girl or boy by this method is 60 to 70 percent.

IVF techniques have successfully cloned many animals. Prometea (in the foreground) was the first cloned horse. The DNA of a skin cell taken from Stella Cometa (background) was fused with an enucleated egg from another horse. The resulting embryo was implanted in Stella Cometa's uterus. Prometea was born in May 2003. Stella Cometa is Prometea's surrogate mother—but both horses share the same DNA and are also identical twins.

IVF and genetic engineering

Scientists can use techniques similar to those used in IVF to manipulate the genes of plants and animals in order to make them grow and develop in different ways. This is called genetic engineering. For example, scientists can remove the DNA from the egg of an animal and replace it with DNA from another organism. The new DNA might contain an extra gene that makes the newly created animal resistant to a certain disease.

In humans, genetic engineering could one day help treat fertility problems or cure genetic diseases. For example, a faulty gene found in an early embryo could be "fixed" or replaced by a normal version of the gene.

IVF and cloning

IVF-type methods can also be used in cloning. A clone is a living organism that is genetically identical to another. Cloning researchers make use of many techniques originally developed for IVF, such as creating conditions that allow early embryos to grow in a laboratory before being put back in the uterus. Many plants and animals have already been cloned.

In humans, cloning combined with stem cell technology (*see sidebar, below*) may allow some of a person's cells to be taken and "grown" into new tissues and organs in order to treat a future health problem in that person. At present, the research and practice of human cloning is banned in many countries.

IVF and stem cells

The "spare" embryos from IVF are a potential source of stem cells. Stem cells—unlike most cells in the human body, such as muscle or blood cells—are undifferentiated. Stem cells have the potential to become other types of cell and may therefore have future medical applications. Undifferentiated cells could be used to grow tissues such as skin and muscle—and even organs such as a liver or heart—from a person's own stem cells. Then, if the person develops, say kidney failure, a new tissue or organ could be grown and implanted to treat the problem with no risk of rejection.

The stem cells within early embryos created by IVF are even more useful to researchers than adult stem cells. All mature organs have some stem cells available for repairing that organ, so most adult stem cells can only develop into a particular type of cell, while embryonic stem cells can develop into any kind of cell.

Laws regarding the use of IVF embryos for stem cell research vary from one country to another. Some countries ban their use in any stem cell or cloning research. Others allow the use of embryos up to a certain stage of development, such as four- or eight-cell embryos.

CUTTING EDGE   DEBATES

Embryonic stem cells

The use of embryonic stem cells for medical research has stirred much public debate. Is it right to use an embryo with the potential to develop into a human being as a source of material for stem cell research? What if that research leads to treatments that could improve health care practices and save many lives? What do you think?

CHAPTER 7

Funding, Ethics, and Laws

IVF not only helps people have babies—it is also big business. The IVF "business" includes researchers, doctors, nurses, support staff, and fertility hospitals and clinics—and also requires many kinds of medical equipment and technologies. Besides these frontline people and assets, the business is supported by large quantities of related informational, educational, and legal material. Any couple participating in IVF treatment can expect to pay out thousands of dollars.

In the United States, IVF treatments cost between $3,000 and $20,000 per cycle (chance for success), depending on a number of factors, including the reputation of the clinic and the "quality" of the frozen donor eggs or sperm. ("Quality" depends on the age and health of the donors.) In Britain, the cost of IVF is not as variable—in 2005, the price for IVF was about $5,600 per cycle in U.S. dollars.

Who pays for IVF?

The majority of IVF treatment is paid for by the people hoping to conceive a child. In some countries, such as Australia, people sometimes obtain a gift, loan, or grant from a charity or from the government or may carry an insurance policy for IVF treatment. After a number of years of treatments but no children, the insurance company pays the costs of the treatments.

In the United States, IVF is only available to those who can pay for it privately. A few health insurance plans cover the costs of IVF, but most health insurers refuse to cover treatments for IVF. The IVF procedure is considered an "elective" treatment, like cosmetic surgery—not a life-or-death problem.

In England, most IVF is paid for privately. Only a tiny proportion is paid for by the government-funded National Health Service

The first IVF court case

What could have been the first IVF pregnancy, in 1973, instead turned into the first of many IVF court cases. In New York City, Dr. William Sweeney and Dr. Landrum Shettles removed eggs from patient Doris Del-Zio and mixed them in a test tube with sperm from her husband, John. The following day, the doctors' senior boss, Raymond Vande Wiele stopped the process. In 1974, the Del-Zios started a court case against Vande Wiele, claiming $1.5 million in damages. The case was settled four years later when the Del-Zios received $50,000. In 1983, Vande Wiele became a director of New York City's first IVF clinic.

IVF has been at the center of a number of legal disputes. In 2003, two women in England, Natallie Evans (right) and Lorraine Hadley (left) went to court to try to save frozen embryos—conceived with their former partners—from being destroyed. The former partners had withdrawn consent for the use of the embryos in IVF treatment. The women lost in court.

(NHS). New guidelines established in England in 2005 state that couples who meet certain conditions will receive three cycles of IVF treatment paid for by the NHS. Couples must be childless, younger than thirty-five years, in good general health, and with no family history of certain genetic illnesses.

The ethics of IVF

The governments of most countries monitor IVF procedures, establish codes of practice, and ensure that IVF is carried out safely and to high ethical standards. Practitioners of IVF are also bound by national, regional, and state laws.

In the United States, IVF is controlled by the American Society for Reproductive Medicine (ASRM) and the Centers for Disease Control (CDC). In Australia, the National Health and Medical Research Council (NHMRC) oversees IVF.

In England, the process of monitoring IVF began with the Human Fertility and Embryology Act of 1990. The Human Fertility and Embryology Authority (HFEA) was established in 1991 to oversee IVF and other forms of assisted reproduction, as well as IVF applications such as research into stem cells and cloning.

International organizations include the European Society for Human Reproduction and Embryology (ESHRE) and the International Federation of Fertility Societies (IFFS). Both of these organizations coordinate information about the latest developments in IVF from around the world and provide summaries to IVF clients and practitioners, as well as to governmental and regional bodies.

Rights and wrongs

IVF remains a controversial technique for many people and has been the subject of fierce disagreement. Anti-IVF protesters often cite moral or religious objections to the practice. Many do not believe that humans have the right to interfere in what is seen as

CUTTING EDGE   FACTS

IVF tourism

The laws on IVF vary greatly from country to country. In some countries in the Middle East, IVF is illegal. Other countries, such as Hungary and Slovenia, allow many forms of IVF, and clinics are often unregulated. Most countries' policies are somewhere beween these extremes. They permit IVF, but with strict controls that make it as safe and effective as possible. Since the mid-1990s, these variations between countries have led to a booming international business in "IVF tourism." People seeking IVF treatment often have pre-IVF tests in their own country (if such tests are not illegal there). They then travel abroad, perhaps even taking the frozen or fresh samples of eggs and sperm with them, to have the IVF treatment. People also decide to travel abroad for IVF for economic reasons. Prices vary considerably around the globe. In 2005, the cost of an IVF cycle in India could be less than one-fifth of its cost in the United States.

God's will. Some argue that any fertilized egg or early embryo is a potential human being with certain human rights. They disagree with the way IVF teams can simply discard unused embryos.

Other people support IVF and promote further research into this field. They focus on the great joy IVF has brought to couples who, without this procedure, would have had no chance of becoming parents. Companies with interests in IVF, such as drug companies and medical equipment manufacturers, also add their voices to the debate. Protesters and supporters pressure their legislators and government authorities to change the laws and regulations that govern IVF.

U.S. president George W. Bush at a White House ceremony in July 2006. He congratulated families who adopted frozen embryos (referred to as "snowflake babies") left over from other couples' attempts to conceive through IVF. Bush holds Jack Jones, a so-called "snowflake baby."

CHAPTER 8

IVF and the Future

IVF is now a well-established medical technique, and, although only about one in four or five IVF cycles is successful, success rates are gradually improving.

The long-term effects of IVF have defied the predictions of its early opponents. The majority of IVF babies are healthy, and there is no evidence to suggest that IVF has led to a breakdown of family life—although IVF has given rise to some unusual kinds of family (*see Chapter 4*).

Current and future trends

IVF is an evolving science. The technology is continually being tested and monitored as part of ongoing efforts to improve the safety and success rate of IVF procedures. Research into various aspects of IVF helps refine the techniques.

Medical experts advise against the multiple embryo transfer, or MET (placing two or three early embryos into the uterus) technique. The current trend in IVF is toward single embryo transfer, or SET, in order to diminish the health risks to the mother and to her fetus.

CUTTING EDGE   SCIENCE

Signaling substance
In 2005, researchers working with mice discovered a "signaling substance" called lysophosphatidic acid (LPA). The LPA promotes the ability of the fertilized egg to implant itself into the lining of the uterus. Drugs that mimic or boost the effect of LPA might increase the chances of implanting as part of IVF.

The use of ICSI for IVF, in which a sperm is injected directly into the egg, is increasing. In some IVF centers, ICSI has replaced "traditional" IVF, in which eggs and sperm are mixed in laboratory dishes before implantation.

Researchers are also investigating new ways of making IVF safer and more effective. Future ICSI methods might include pretreating sperm to make fertilization more likely—for example, by breaking the sperm's acrosome (*see sidebar, page 32*). Other researchers are devising drugs and methods that encourage implantation in the uterine wall (*see sidebar, page 54*).

As IVF has become more widespread and established as a business, IVF centers work toward making their services more convenient and customer friendly. Prospective parents often discuss their options in office-like settings, and appointments are set up to accommodate their schedules.

Two microneedles are inserted into a droplet of semen to capture fertile sperm, using a method known as CISS (computer imaging sperm selection). The sperm, viewed through a video microscope, are selected by a computer for their fertility, based on their tail movement: More vigorous tail movements signal faster, stronger the sperm—all the more likely to fertilize an egg.

Pre-implantation genetic diagnosis (PGD)

One of the biggest growth areas in IVF is pre-implantation genetic diagnosis (PGD). With PGD, one or two cells are taken from the early embryos at about the eight-cell stage, shortly after fertilization. The DNA in the cells is tested for genetic problems. During testing, the embryos are kept alive in dishes. Following the tests, only one embryo—the one that appears the healthiest—is placed in the uterus.

The PGD was developed in the early 1990s. Its first application was for detecting genetic defects, such as Duchenne muscular dystrophy and Down syndrome. Rapid progress in the science of genetics has greatly increased the number of genetic problems that can be detected by PGD. Constant improvements in genetic technology expands the list of genetic defects that PGD can identify. The technique can also detect an embryo's sex (*see pages 46–47*).

PGD is used in cases where standard IVF may not be safe or successful. For example, it may be used if there is a history of a genetic disease in the family, or for women who are older. Women who have not become pregnant after several IVF cycles or who have already had more than one miscarriage (an abrupt, natural expulsion of a fetus that has died in utero) also benefit from PGD.

By the end of 2005, more than five thousand babies came into the world thanks to PGD. An ongoing European survey monitors about two hundred children born after IVF and PGD. Most are now in their teens. By the mid-2000s, these children appeared to be developing in much the same way as other children.

The use of PGD is increasing annually. A 2005 report suggested that PGD might soon even become a routine method in IVF. In standard IVF, early embryos are usually selected on the basis of

CUTTING EDGE   SCIENCE

Predicting problems

PGD may also be used as a predictor of problems with IVF. If all the embryos from one IVF cycle are found to have genetic disorders, this suggests the same could happen for the next IVF attempt. It could indicate that IVF for the woman in question will never be successful. This knowledge—while very disappointing—might prevent further effort and heartbreat, as well as save time and money.

appearance—the number of cells, their apparent health, and their overall shape. According to the 2005 report, however, even normal-looking embryos sometimes carry genetic or chromosomal defects. Genetic problems occur not only with embryos from the eggs of older women, but also in those from younger women. One study revealed that nearly 75 percent of eight hundred early embryos carried chromosomal disorders.

An IVF human embryo undergoing PGD. The eight-celled embryo is being held by a pipette (*left*) so that a smaller pipette (*right*) can break the embryo membrane and remove one of the cells for genetic screening.

Pre-implantation genetic haplotyping (PGH)

In 2006, a team of researchers in England announced a new version of PGD known as pre-implantation genetic haplotyping (PGH). Instead of screening cells from an early embryo for just one or two specific genetic defects, PGH examines a single, designated chromosome for particular "markers" known to occur with faulty genes. The technique, called multiple displacement amplification, or MDA (*see page 58*), quickly produces many copies of the questionable genes for testing. In one screening, the MDA method helps identify many more types of genetic problems than PGD.

Multiple displacement amplification (MDA)

In 2004, researchers developed a new technique called multiple displacement amplification (MDA). The MDA process allows reachers to produce millions of copies of DNA from one embryonic cell. When used alongside PGD, the MDA technique increases the accuracy of identifying faulty genes. In 2005, researchers in Spain used both MDA and PGD to separate the healthy embryos from those fertilized with sperm that carried a genetic disease called Marfan syndrome. Marfan syndrome causes curvature of the spine, joint and muscle weakness, and other problems.

IVF and "designer babies"

In a sense, many "designer babies" already exist. They are the babies, who—as early embryos—were screened and selected by PGD to ensure freedom from genetic diseases. So far, PGD has been used only for medical purposes, but in the future, PGD may also be used for other reasons. PGD makes possible the selection of early embryos with genes that feature a specific skin or hair color, control the adult height of that baby, and that indicate a certain level of intelligence. While this type of genetic engineering is theoretically and technically possible, the process brings with it profound moral and social implications. People with financial advantages would be more likely to afford such treatment, which—in the distant future—would result in sharply divided, unequal societies.

CUTTING EDGE MOMENTS

The first "designer baby"

In August 2000, worldwide headlines hailed Adam Nash as the first IVF "designer baby." In fact, he had been born using PGD to select one embryo of fifteen embryos to ensure that he did not carry the gene for a rare blood disease called Fanconi's anemia. He was also considered a "savior sibling"—stem cells from his umbilical cord were used to treat his sister Molly, who has Fanconi's anemia.

Personal organ banks

The creation of personal organ banks for IVF children is another future advantage of the technology. It is possible to split an early IVF

embryo and freeze some of its stem cells for future use while allowing the remaining cells of the embryo to develop into a baby. In the future, it may be possible to use these embryonic stem cells to grow tissues and organs in the laboratory. If that person someday requires a tissue or organ transplant, he or she would have genetically perfect transplant material available.

Molly Nash, who suffers from a rare blood disease, with her "savior sibling," Adam. Stem cells from Adam's umbilical cord helped boost Molly's immune system and saved her life.

When present is past

Compared to the controversy caused by the birth of Louise Brown in 1978, IVF today is an accepted procedure. It is relatively safe and becoming more routine for couples who cannot conceive in the natural way. Today, the focus for debate in medical ethics has moved onto newer fields such as stem cell research and cloning. Medical science will undoubtedly continue to make advances in technology and stir up new ethical questions. Fifty years from now, however, people may look back at the early history of IVF and marvel that the procedures ever caused controversy.

Glossary

abortion The end a pregnancy caused by the removal of a fetus from the uterus.

acrosome The front end, or "cap," of a sperm cell that pushes against and through the outer membrane of an egg cell during fertilization.

AI (artificial insemination) The placement of sperm cells into a woman's body through artificial procedures.

ARTs (assisted reproductive technologies) A range of techniques for helping people have children when they cannot do so naturally.

biological mother/father The parent who provides the genetic material (egg or sperm, respectively) for the conception of a child.

cervix The narrow opening or "neck" of the uterus.

chromosomes Short strings of DNA (genetic material) that form during cell division.

clone An exact genetic copy of another living organism (plant or animal).

corpus luteum A small, yellowish lump that forms from the empty follicle in the ovary after the release of a ripe egg; it produces female hormones as part of the menstrual cycle.

DNA (deoxyribonucleic acid) The genetic material that contains the coded information needed to produce a living organism.

ectopic pregnancy The implantation and subsequent development of a fertilized egg outside the uterus, usually in a fallopian tube.

egg A female reproductive cell.

embryo An early stage of development, from implantation in the uterine wall to about eight weeks after fertilization.

endometrium The blood-rich lining of the uterus that encourages implantation and nourishes the embryo.

fallopian tube The tube that carries a woman's ripe egg to her uterus; it is the usual site of fertilization during natural conception.

fertile Capable of reproducing.

fertility drug General name for a group of medications taken by a woman to increase the chances of production of ripe eggs.

fertilization The moment of joining a sperm with an egg that can eventually develop into a baby.

fetus The term for an unborn baby from eight weeks of development to birth.

follicle A temporary, fluid-filled structure in a woman's ovary that contains a ripening egg cell.

fraternal Twins or other multiple siblings that develop at the same time from separate eggs.

genes A section of DNA that carries the instructions for the development of specific traits in an organism.

GIFT (gamete intra-fallopian tube transfer) A variation of IVF in which eggs and sperm are collected and placed into the woman's fallopian tube in order for fertilization to take place.

hormone A chemical "messenger" that travels through the blood to affect cells around the body.

ICSI (intra-cytoplasmic sperm injection) A variation on IVF in which a single sperm cell is injected into the interior of an egg cell.

implantation The sinking of the fertilized egg into the lining of the uterus.

inherited disease An illness or health problem that is passed from parents to offspring through the genes.

in vitro A Latin term meaning "in glass," used generally in medicine to mean something that happens in artificial conditions.

IVF (in vitro fertilization) A process in which eggs and sperm are joined artificially to produce a baby.

laparoscope A telescope-like medical device that is inserted into the body through a small incision (cut) to view internal organs or perform surgery.

menopause A time in a woman's life when her menstrual cycle becomes erratic and stops; she no longer produces ripe eggs and can no longer have a baby by natural means.

menstrual cycle The series of changes in a woman's body that occur roughly once a month and cause the ripening and release of an egg from an ovary, as well as a thickening of the lining of the uterus—in preparation for conceiving a baby.

MET (multiple embryo transfer) The placing of more than one embryo (and often two or three) into the uterus as part of IVF.

miscarriage The natural, unintended death of a fetus and its explusion from the uterus.

nucleus The "control center" of a cell; contains the DNA for that organism.

OHSS (ovarian hyperstimulation syndrome) A group of health problems that develop in some women who have taken fertility drugs.

ovaries Reproductive organs in women; each contains thousands of egg cells, one of which ripens once a month as part of the menstrual cycle.

postmenopausal The time in a woman's life after menopause when she can no longer conceive a child through natural means.

PID (pelvic inflammatory disease) A general name for infections and other problems that cause inflammation of the reproductive and urinary organs in a woman's pelvis (lower abdomen).

savior sibling The term for a child (usually conceived by IVF), who can provide body parts (such as bone marrow) to treat the illness of a brother or sister.

semen A thick, milky fluid produced by a man's reproductive organs and glands; it contains sperm cells, nutrients, and other substances.

SET (single embryo transfer) The placing of a single embryo into the uterus as part of IVF.

sperm A male reproductive cell.

stem cells Undifferentiated (nonspecialized) cells that have the potential to divide and develop into many different cells.

surrogate mother A woman who bears a child for an infertile couple.

testicles Two egg-shaped reproductive organs in a skin bag (scrotum) below a male's abdomen; each testicle produces millions of sperm daily.

TET (tubal embryo transfer) A variation on IVF in which eggs and sperm are put into an artificial container for fertilization—as in standard IVF—and are allowed to develop to the early embryo stage before implantation in the fallopian tube.

urethra The tube that carries urine (liquid waste) from the bladder out of the body, and, in men, also carries sperm along the penis and out of the body.

uterus The muscular organ in a woman's lower abdomen that can expand to accommodate and nourish a developing fetus.

vas deferens In men, the tube that carries sperm cells from the testes, to another tube, the urethra.

ZIFT (zygote intra-fallopian tube transfer) A variation on IVF in which eggs and sperm are put into an artificial container for fertilization—as in standard IVF—and then the fertilized egg (known as a zygote) is placed in the woman's fallopian tube.

Further Information

BOOKS

Dowswell, Paul. *Genetic Engineering*. 21st Century Issues (series). World Almanac® Library (2005).

Graham, Ian. *Genetics: The Study of Heredity*. Investigating Science (series). Gareth Stevens Publishing (2002).

Macdonald, Fiona. *The First "Test Tube Baby."* Days That Changed the World (series). World Almanac® Library (2004).

Orr, Tamra B. *Test Tube Babies*. Science on the Edge (series). Blackbirch Press (2003).

Woolf, Alex. *History of Medicine: Medicine in the Twentieth Century and Beyond*. Enchanted Lion Books (2006).

Zach, Kim K. *Reproductive Technology*. Great Medical Discoveries (series). Lucent Books (2004).

WEB SITES

www.pbs.org/wgbh/nova/genome/explore.html
Explore a stretch of the human genome.

https://www3.nationalgeographic.com/genographic/population.html
Click on the numbers in the upper right corner of the Web site for a short tutorial on the effects of genes on human development.

www.pbs.org/wgbh/nova/baby/18ways.html
Discover information on at least eighteen different procedures that help people become parents using various methods of assisted reproduction and IVF.

www.genetics.gsk.com/kids/heredity01.htm
Learn how physical traits get passed from parents to offspring.

Publisher's note to educators and parents: Our editors have carefully reviewed these Web sites to ensure that they are suitable for children. Many Web sites change frequently, however, and we cannot guarantee that a site's future contents will continue to meet our high standards of quality and educational value. Be advised that children should be closely supervised whenever they access the Internet.

Index

Index *(continued)*